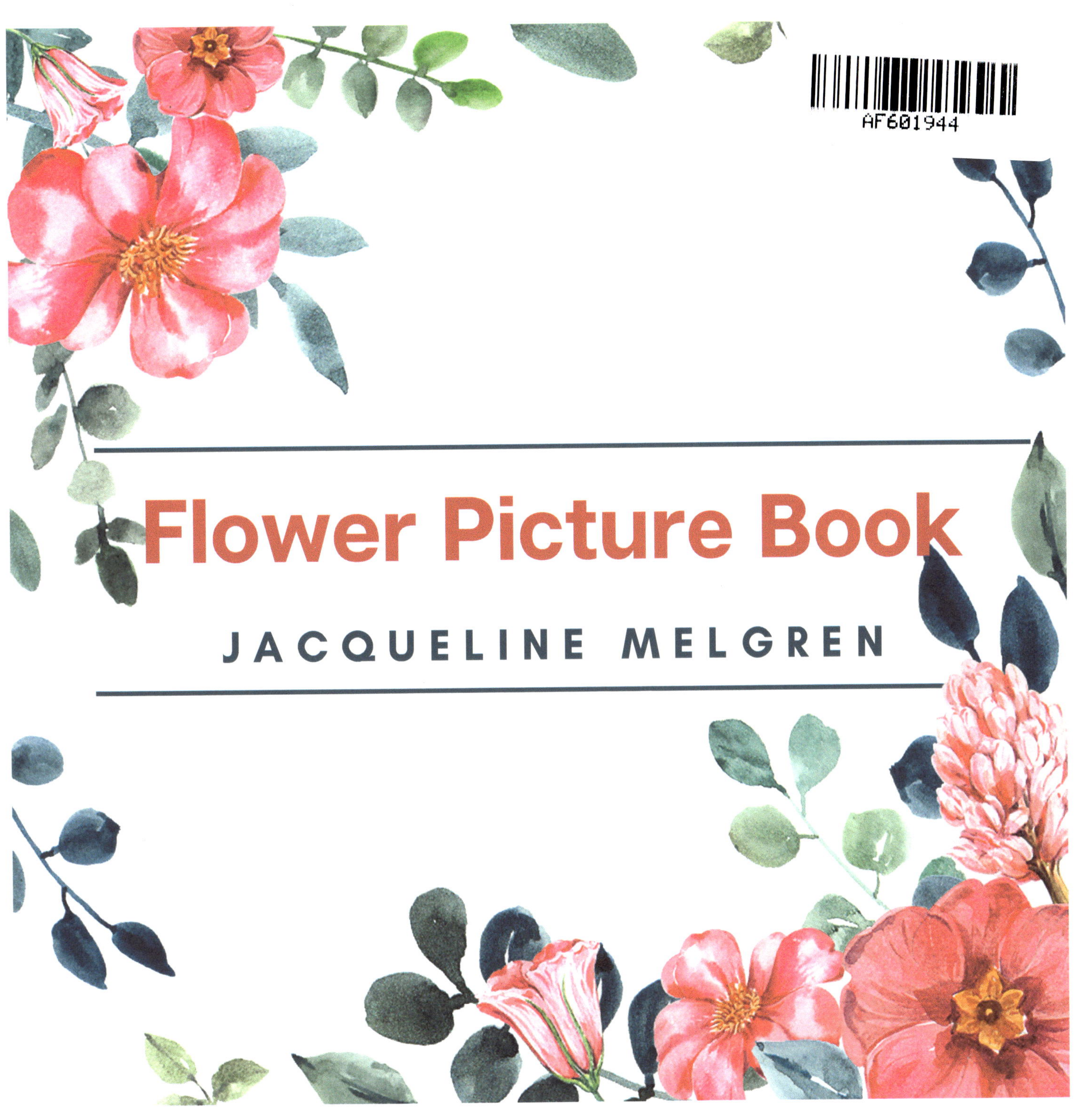

Flower Picture Book

JACQUELINE MELGREN

Begonia

Daffodil

Carnations

Dahlia

Gerbera Daisy

Pansies

Tulips

Geranium

Rose

Hydrangea

Marigold

Gladioli

Orchid

Vinca

Chrysanthemum

Hibiscus

Kalanchoe

Easter Lily

Cyclamen

Hyacinth

Iris

Aster

Freesia

Sunflower

Coneflower

Buttercup

Calibrachoa

Gardenia

Coleus

Peony

African Violet

Thank
you!

www.ingramcontent.com/pod-product-compliance
Ingram Content Group UK Ltd.
Pitfield, Milton Keynes, MK11 3LW, UK
UKHW060113300726
14090UKWH00002B/167

* 9 7 8 9 1 8 9 4 5 2 4 7 3 *